HIVE

THE BRITTINGHAM PRIZE IN POETRY

HIVE

CHRISTINA STODDARD

The University of Wisconsin Press

Publication of this volume has been made possible, in part, through support from the Brittingham Fund.

The University of Wisconsin Press
1930 Monroe Street, 3rd Floor
Madison, Wisconsin 53711-2059
uwpress.wisc.edu

3 Henrietta Street, Covent Garden
London WC2E 8LU, United Kingdom
eurospanbookstore.com

Library of Congress Cataloging-in-Publication Data

Stoddard, Christina, author.
 [Poems. Selections]
 Hive / Christina Stoddard.
    pages   cm — (The Brittingham prize in poetry)
 ISBN 978-0-299-30424-9 (pbk. : alk. paper) — ISBN 978-0-299-30423-2 (e-book)
 I. Title. II. Series: Brittingham prize in poetry (Series).
 PS3619.T6397A6   2015
 811'.6—dc23
                      2014030781

CONTENTS

III

ACKNOWLEDGMENTS

I am grateful to the editors of the journals in which these poems, or earlier versions of them, first appeared:

DIAGRAM: "How to Make Up for Unhealthy Habits"
The Pinch: "Abby's Mother Shows Us Where Ted Bundy Signed Her Yearbook"
Slipstream: "Maureen"
storySouth: "What It Is to Sin" and "What If God Had Said It Differently"
Tupelo Quarterly: "Bodies of Two Girls Found in Woods," "At Little George's House, the Christmas Lights Stayed Up All Year," "I Am Thinking of Salmon," and "Hive"

I am grateful for the support and encouragement of many people, especially Kendra DeColo, Margy Roark, Elizabeth Townsend, Stephanie Pruitt Gaines, Emily Choate, Gary McDowell, and Lisa Dordal. I thank my family, Kate Coventry, Edward Gibbs, Meredith Hunter, Nikki Klemmer, Emily Stenberg, Rhett Iseman Trull, Fritz Ward, and Roxanne Halpine Ward.

I am profoundly grateful for all my teachers over the years. A special debt of thanks goes to Claudia Emerson, Robert Hass, and Ellen Bryant Voigt, who each gave me the right push at the right time.

To Lucia Perillo, Ron Wallace, and everyone at the University of Wisconsin Press: thank you for making this book possible.

I would also like to thank the staff and board of the Ragdale Foundation, an artists' community where many of these poems were first written.

There are two people without whom this book would not exist. Tanya, thank you for your unfailing belief and for demanding the best from me as a person and as a writer. And above all, Chris: thanks for always having my back. I love you.

I

Bodies of Two Girls Found in Woods

The sharp ruin of flies. A chilly morning
next to the river where steelhead spawn.
Sunlight bright as a railroad spike.
Clouds bitten by tamaracks. Wind slicing
the leather throats of frogs.
Sweet gums bruised by woodpeckers.
The slow fat rat of the river
gnawing at twenty cold toes.

Party Where Maureen Pierced Everyone's Ears

The one Jane came to. It was ballsy of Maureen
       to invite her, since Jane lived
           in the North End. But Maureen did

         what she wanted—the deep end
    of the pool, the rides home from Robert's
friends. When Rita said her cousin said

you could tattoo with ink
       from a ballpoint, Maureen bet on it
          and Rita held out her ankle.

        By the time Maureen returned
    with ice cubes and her mother's lighter,
Abby wanted her cartilage pierced. I was

the assistant in fishnets. I would not let the needle
       enter me—no more doors in my body
          forced open. And I knew

        Maureen would keep the others
    from making fun. I held Rita's leg
while Maureen drew a little heart.

She unscrewed the pen, exposed the well.
        Rita took the needle without making
                a sound. After Abby's turn,

                Jane asked for the box and chose
        a tiny gold stud. I clipped her hair
behind her temple and held the ice to her lobe.

Rita showed the heart to everyone
        in Social Studies and Shane went crazy
                for it, hands traveling

                between her ankle
        and the frayed threads where her jeans ripped
at the knee. There was a rumor that Shane

knifed a man in the neck. He asked Rita to meet him
        near the band annex after school.
                She had wanted that for a long time.

This Time the Marina

Half laughing, we duck under the clipped chain link,
onto spray-slick rocks. We slip past

the pitched shine of the pleasure boats
to find the path leading higher up.

His flask, my mimicked sips.
A frenzy of fireworks for the minor league.

I open his bag of lychees. Use my nails
to circle the stem and expose the fruit.
Flush when he applauds.

He always calls last minute. Silver sedan,
windshield with a jagged crack.

We inspect the stars through a telescope
he says he borrowed. There are worlds

out there after all, coiled tight
as copper wire. He drives me home
past the burned-out hulk of a minivan

that has wintered on the corner lot.
On my porch, hydrangea blooms

crowd the railing. I run my hand over them
and petals fall like bruises. He is
still watching me, another broken rule.

The Oxford Unabridged

was how I learned the word *fellatio*,
though I paused to look up *orgasm*
and my understanding of *male genitals* was abstract
at best. I had read the word fellatio in the newspaper,
Local section, in a story
about three runaways, two boys and a girl.
A man held them in a cabin
for two weeks. He raped the girl
and forced the boys to perform fellatio on him
repeatedly. I didn't have to look up *rape*—
I'd known that word since fourth grade
when Takeisha told me
that her uncle took off his pants
when he babysat and we told
our teacher. But I read
the definition of fellatio
and I considered what I knew
about *repeatedly*.
The man picked up the kids
hitching on the freeway
and said he'd take them as far
as Enumclaw. The girl
gave her testimony yesterday,
which sounded strange when I read it
because in our church,
testimony was when we all stood up

to bear witness of Christ
on the first Sunday, in lieu of a sermon.
The article said the girl had a glass eye.
The man stabbed out her real one
when she tried to escape. The man
told her: I will not kill you. I will
take some things away.

At Little George's House, the Christmas Lights Stayed Up All Year

If I hadn't been grounded, I would have wandered
with Rita and LeShawndra down Sprague Avenue.
After getting kicked out of Pinch's Deli,
we would've pooled our nickels
for a four-pack of Twinkies from the Hostess outlet
and cased the middle school for something to do.
I would have lost to Rita again
in the game to pitch rocks against the gym's
highest window. If I could aim better, I wouldn't
have hit Ms. Wilson's windshield and gotten grounded,
and then we all would have been poking around the edge
of the fenced-off baseball field
when Little George walked by with his yellow mutt.
If Rita hadn't wanted to be a veterinarian,
she wouldn't have been so eager to see George's new
pet rabbit. LeShawndra might not have gone along
but her grandmother's house smelled of mothballs
and wounds. Had I not been confined
to my yard, I would have followed them down the steps
into George's dim-lit basement. We'd been there
before. I would have stroked the trembling baby rabbit's
spine. I would have been with them when George
went upstairs to get a carrot, locked the door,
and set the match.

I Am Thinking of Salmon

I am thinking of salmon
because I am thinking of breeding.
I am thinking of breeding
because I've turned thirty-four
and the bellies of my friends
keep announcing themselves.
I am thinking of breeding
because I have crossed that line
where I say "men" more often than "guys"
and I've found one who sleeps next to me
and shops with me for apples and bread.
I am thinking of salmon
because I used to watch them spawn
in the Puyallup River, in White River,
in all the smaller streams where I hiked
with my sisters and we would stop to watch
their silvery pink skins glinting.
I am thinking of salmon,
how they will do anything to return home,
but I'm not like that. I cannot stand
my home—the mildewed building
where my parents still live,
same neighbors for decades
because the houses don't sell.
I am thinking of breeding
because I've left that street

forever. But I think of that street
more often lately; it intrudes on my work
and on my quiet moments
and I fall silent in conversation
when I remember the doll house
my mother made out of cardboard
and the gingham scraps she sewed into curtains
because I begged for the dream house
from the commercial.
I am thinking of salmon because
when I was young, before my father
took out a second mortgage
on the house no one would buy,
we used to eat salmon. Whole fish
from Johnny's, a shed
with an old-fashioned cash register
whose punch-buttons rang like bells,
where the fishermen would pull their boats
up to the dock out back
and you could take your pick
from the wriggling pile in the hold.
I am thinking of salmon
because it's impossible to get the good stuff
where I live now, a place I arrived at
without really meaning to.
Here the salmon is tasteless
and farmed, a shade of pink
that I know is falsified

because I've seen real salmon,
I've fished for real salmon. The first salmon
I caught when I was seven or eight.
My uncle showed me how to slit its belly
to clean it, and when I slid my knife through—
he said *Don't be so gentle*, said
you can't hurt it—I opened its stomach
to find weird slick little beads inside.
Roe, my uncle said, and I didn't know what
that meant, so without thinking
he said *Eggs, she was pregnant*.
And I cried. I keep thinking
of this salmon while I keep thinking
about breeding. I've caught lots of other salmon
and never found roe again.
I am thinking about home while Lisa and I
meet for lunch. Her belly
is so big she knocks over the salt
and I'm not sure whether I want this
for myself. I think about swimming
against the river. I think about
what I would do with a daughter.
I consider my job and I consider
leaving my job. I could not trust strangers
with my child. Not after what happened to me
as a child. How tired Lisa looks,
but how happy. And again how tired.
I think of the terrible things this life requires

of us. I think about how my parents believe
that we all lived with God in a pre-mortal life,
before our souls received physical bodies
on Earth. They believe
that every child birthed on this planet
was first a soul up in heaven
selecting its parents. I'm not Mormon
anymore but I cannot help
imagining my daughter looking down,
crossing her fingers that I will say yes,
waiting to be born.
The salmon don't have to prepare,
paint a room in the house, buy a crib.
They swim in the direction
they are pulled. They just go.

Hive

I have that dream again where the Elders
        stand mute in their suits and ties.
            They circle around

and place their hands on my head. They push me
        into the earth, into the slatted box
            that is waiting. A secret box

filled with bees. Now a host, I gag
        on buzz and clack. The box bobs up
            in the waters of a baptismal font

mounted on the backs of twelve oxen. The bees
        have sealed us inside with wax.
            I try to ask for some music

at the end of the world, but my mouth
        fills with swarm. Then I hear
            the Elders singing

"Know This, That Every Soul
        Is Free," while I am stung
            the purple of reverent hearts.

The Profession of the Whale

Among all creatures,
        the birds and the horse
do not sin. Fish of the sea

        do not sin. Only the hearts of men
            pump anger in,
        cowardice out.

        This talker
quakes on my tongue, helpless
        in the reeking dark. Why shouldn't I
let the weeds in my teeth slap
            his derelict ankles? For I

        am havoc. I am ruin
beneath their ships, ready
        to breach,

but God is yielding. Each time a prophet
        is lashed to the mast
by his brothers, head hanging limp
            in the heat,
        God sends me

to stir the water. To show the sinners
                my monstrous jaw.
As the storm around us worsens,
I ready my funeral song—

        but the men tremble,
loose their captive, and God
      so pities the work
of His hands.

          Now I cantillate
     to the deserter in my belly
so that he too
      will cry unto his Lord.

Like all men, he believes being spared
      means that he is loved.

Jacks

I'm facedown on the porch
where I threw myself
as soon as the lowrider
turned up its bass. And now

Maureen is tugging my arm
and saying something,
but I am deaf
and when did
the bullets stop? Maureen

motions again and we scramble
inside. My forearm is studded
with jacks. I pick them out
and get a rag for the weeping.
We lift the green bedsheet
that covers the front window
and peer down the street.
No one has come out
of their house. No one comes out
until Juan's mother,

whose wailing breaks
like an egg in a pan. She keeps
lifting the hem of her sweatshirt
to her face,

exposing her belly
to the empty yards. Behind her
Juan's uncles carry a girl
in a dark blue shirt. Raquel.
They all get into Ernesto's
car. But Juan isn't here. He
must have known.

      Maureen and I rehearse what we will say
      when the cops show up. For hours
      we're pinned in the living room,
      watching the nothing that happens.

Past nine, Maureen goes to the kitchen
to make macaroni and cheese.
I am sleeping over so my mother
knows nothing. I have
the rest of my life to keep silent.
We take our bowls
back to the porch, listen
to crane flies sizzling
in the streetlights,
and begin again
with onesies.

Abby's Mother Shows Us Where Ted Bundy Signed Her Yearbook

She goes right to the page
        where he's written
Hi Lydia,
        the letters
tight as fists on a steering wheel.

        In the picture, he's my age.
He walked through my school. Its white tile,
        its doorknobs. Ted

        who liked
to swing into the skull.
        Forward again with both
arms round.

But before that. Before he
opened the telescope
        of his hands.
The message says *Nice knowing you.*

In a cartoon my sister loves
        to watch, Ben Franklin
courts storms

with his kite,
              and when he is struck

        his body keeps changing
from jagged bolt to flesh
              and back again.
The buzz is funny. The shaking legs.

        Baptized Ted, faith thin
as a wire. Valiant Ted.
        Ted of the fraudulent sling
on his arm, struggling with books
        when a brunette walks by—
                      her kindness
        a mouth of its own.

              Ted with the guileless
smile. Ted who didn't flinch.

        He kept some of them alive,
        for a while. In the woods

whose trees I know.
        Their skin unpeeling
        into darkness and clodded ground.

Maureen

Maybe if you had stood aiming
a real enough crossbow
at a man twice your size
and told him you'd kill him
if he ever came back, you too
would fall that night
into dreamless sleep.
When you woke, you might
eat ice cream for breakfast. Watch
for new cars on your street
and more neighbors selling crack
from their basements. You might
invite me, the skinny Mormon girl,
to play cards on your front porch
in total defiance of Juan
next door, who says he'll get a piece
of your ass someday,
and chicks say they don't want it,
but everyone loves a good fuck.
You would borrow five dollars
from Mrs. Edwards,
the fat woman across the street,
and walk to Safeway
to buy a steak to hold against
your pregnant mother's purple eye.

I Ask My Father If the Green River Killer's Victims Go to Heaven

Because we are not equally loved on this earth,
because we are all God's children,
in the temple we baptize

lists of the dead. It is why
I step into the font, white dress
dragging like sailcloth.

An Elder takes both wrists
and pushes my body underwater
while saying a stranger's name.

In the water, I'm supposed to go absent.

I baptize you in the name of Lynette Snyder, who is dead
In the name of the Father, the Son, and the Holy Ghost

As I go under, I glimpse
the howling green river,
the parade of persuaded girls.

I see you, I tell them. I know
you are here.

I baptize you in the name of Karen Haskill, who is dead
In the name of the Father, the Son, and the Holy Ghost

Fifty times I drown.

I baptize you in the name of Melissa Porter, who is dead
In the name of the Father, the Son, and the Holy Ghost

I am weightless, light as a nest.
To save the others, the Elder
has to hold me down.

II

Fifteen Girls

The youth camp leader brings in a box
of donuts. Says to the girl who is always picked last
Do you want one? Twenty sit-ups
and it's yours. Becky

pauses and says Okay. She huffs out nineteen,
twenty. Now Sister Barrett asks Laura
Do you want one?
Laura starts to get down on the floor
but Sister Barrett

puts out a hand. Turns to Becky.
Will you do the sit-ups for
Laura's donut? The air
begins to shrink. Becky's face

is about to pop
but she makes it. Her breath ragged
and wheezing. Eighteen,
nineteen, twenty. Sister Barrett
is calm: Will you

do twenty more for each girl?
Maureen tries to stop it, says
We get it, let her go.
We are crying—the circle of girls,

Becky in the middle like an animal,
her pudgy knees knocked together.
Sister Barrett makes us
count aloud. She says This isn't even close
to what your Lord Jesus suffered

for you. Twenty more. Then twenty
after that. Behold
the agony wrought
by your trifling desires.

Help Thou Mine Unbelief

Christ will come from the east, bringing dark
        hosannas. Holiness to the Lord.
Water is rising: it covers truck beds

        and roofs. The devil himself
can appear as an angel of light—every eye
        will see him. We live in the fulness of times,

where temptations multiply like vines. Remember
        from whence thou art fallen.
My sisters and brothers hear the call,

        but I cannot see past my skinned knees.
The body is my favorite room. I have been taught
        to forsake what it asks of me

in the name of redemption. Deny the flesh
        until it starves out like fire.
The Lord knoweth the thoughts of man, that

        they are vanity. The floods
have lifted up, O Lord, the floods lift their voice.
        I will triumph in the works of thy hands.

Appetite

Mormons believe the snake was God's
        plant in the audience. The whole thing

staged, like Andy Kaufman's girlfriend
        challenging him to wrestle.

Without the Fall, my teachers explained,
        Adam and Eve could not have

wed. That's how they sketched it:
        a line between tasting the apple

and becoming husband and wife.
        But if I knew nothing about

the multiplication of bodies into populations,
        I understood that without Eve's sons

I could not be here. The Fall
        made all things in my world possible—

the merry-go-round at Wright Park,
        the ice cream stand on Ruston Way,

my sky blue sweater with shell
        buttons. Whatever its violence

and lies, this place was fixed
        as a two-headed coin. It was

a birthday candle you couldn't blow out.
        And so Eve covered her nakedness.

And every Sunday and Tuesday
        my teachers praised the glory of denial.

They said nothing about appetite
        until it was too late—a year

since insistent kisses
        had consecrated the delicate half-moon

of my neck. It was so easy to be hurt
        by him. To take the body and blood.

Tuesdays at Young Women's Activity Night

This is their time now. Time to hush
your mouth. The Sisters' job is to make you
in a mold that will last until the end of days.
They guide your scissors through old shirts
and the pieces will make you a wedding ring
quilt. And this is what you will teach your children
and your children's children
so that your heart will never vanish from this earth.

Goldfish

Three nights to screw everyone
who wants a turn,
and then you're a Crip.
For life, girl. For life.

I didn't think they'd
do it. But afterward
I hardly saw them
anymore.

      I had homeroom.
      I had lunch.
      My insides crushed.

Kim left lipstick kisses
clotting on the lockers
in the band annex. Outside

the portables, Takeisha's blue jeans
pumped like a heart
as Billy leaned into her. I didn't

mean to watch. I was skipping
to go to Snake Lake.

My mother sat me inside,
fuming—*Those friends of yours*.

I shut my textbook
and chased one of my goldfish
around its tank. Cheap things.
Stupid, bug-eyed.

> I scooped it out so I could see
> what happened.

> I scooped it out so I could watch it
> try.

Each fish netted, one by one,
and emptied onto the rug. I timed
their seizures with a stopwatch.

The record was ninety-three seconds.

> Such struggle.
> Such panic.

The Man Who Built
My Basement Bedroom

who later went to jail for hurting his daughters,
was one of my father's clients

who paid his bill with car repair or landscaping,
cases of cereal still factory-wrapped.

This man was a contractor. In our basement
he put up drywall, white as bandages,

muddy spots at the seams.
He wired plenty of outlets

for my reading lamp and alarm clock.
From the fanned-out paint chips in his hands,

I chose Harbor Blue. He built me
a raised desk with four drawers,

and my father took me shopping
for a secondhand bar-height chair.

An architect's chair, they called it
on the sign. It made me taller.

When I showed the man my books,
he hung shelves of white laminated metal

with brackets I could adjust up and down.
And it was all mine. My first door

with a lock. I wish I could tell you
that after we found out what he did,

I felt the devil's fingerprints
over everything. But I knew—for years

I'd known—that we are encompassed
by demons. We pray to forget their names.

Grandmother Educates Her Darlings

When basting a quilt, smooth out
the batting and center it
before you do anything else.
Hold it straight. No,
not like that.

Crushed cornflakes will stretch
your meatloaf to feed eight
instead of six for the same pound
of ground beef. It's better
than buying the worst cuts
and picking out gristle.

If a can spits at you when pierced
with the opener, throw it out.
That's botulism.

Lemon juice will help
your jam set. A quarter cup
per batch.

When your mother brought
your father to meet us,

he salted the vegetables
before tasting them.
That told me everything
I needed to know.

Westward

Avenge, O Lord, thy slaughtered saints. We fear Missouri nearly lost. Neighbors raise their rifles against us, burn our fields and claim our cattle.

Mobs at Crooked River. Pitch and feathers, boys chained in a row. Skin that grows back as a ragged sack.

In thy book, Lord, record our groans.

By governor's order: *The Mormons must be exterminated.* Our appeals to the Union drift like smoke in the panic. Lawmen break our women like horses.

O Lord, holy and true, we bow to thee with straight backs. They drive us into November blizzards with nothing. Fingers and feet lost to rot.

At Haun's Mill, the militia throws our infants into the well. *Nits make lice.*

On the Dance Floor a Chaperone

taps you on the shoulder
and crooks his finger.
He steers you into an alcove
outside the bishop's office
and points to your sleeves,
which bare too much in his view.
He makes you put on his suit coat
and tells you to get a ride home,
you will have to leave, and you are
trying to keep your face uncrumpled
while you search the hallways
for Maureen because she has your purse
but she's dancing and the chaperone
won't let you back in.
You borrow the coins to call home
even though your father won't get the message
until after the gas money to drive back to Tacoma
has been spent, and when he picks you up
his lecture will last from the Lakewood chapel
all the way to the Sprague Avenue exit.
You are trying not to cry
because of the money
and your father's temper
and the scantness of your sleeves
and in this state Sister Winthrop
finds you waiting for the pay phone

with the brown plaid suit jacket
clutched closed in your fist.
When Sister Winthrop asks what is the matter
you pull the story like tar
from your mouth, and she scoffs.
That's ridiculous, she says, why she
would wear that dress if it came in her size.
She removes the suit coat
and returns it to the chaperone, telling him
the problem has been handled,
and she hides you for the rest of the dance
in the kitchen with her, piping white icing
onto the rims of homemade cookies
for the refreshment table. Sister Winthrop
hands you the droppers of food coloring
but your wrist flicks
produce a hideous grey, which she
retouches quickly with blue.
And when the chaperone
pushes open the kitchen door
to say the punch has run out,
he doesn't even look at you.

Ownership

Don't worry if at first you feel hollow. In the beginning,
      the bones are only a murmur.

Remember, we have a lot invested in you.

As for the body, keep its skin clean. Use soap
      and a scrub of ground walnuts.

Your hands may pray and give alms and dribble
      a basketball.

Your hands may not stray between your legs.

Your mouth delights in taking charge. This is a habit to break.

Your spine on a mattress shows gravity's yoke.

A substantial inheritance.

Your arches might get away from you—
      think of sleep then, of eyelids sewn shut.

Better to shuffle old slippers than wear a funeral shroud.

Even so, your body will starve as long as we want it to.

Try not to scar it. We'd like you to keep it nice.

We've set up the inner workings just right,
	rigged the heart to its wires and hit Go.

If that muscle falters, your body is only meat.

Your breath is a gift. We can take it back.

How to Make Up for Unhealthy Habits

I: PENANCE
Take a vow
of silence. The tongue
a strap, the teeth

a buckle. Get rid of seventy-one percent
of your favorite things.

Set the house on fire
and climb in the bathtub.

II: DISCIPLINE
Holster your panic. Don't believe
every voice you hear.
Yes, you are bobbing like a tire

in a river.
Here is some paper. Fold me a ship. Give it
three masts, historically

accurate rigging. Here is more
paper. Fold me some deckhands. Make
them pants and shirts.

Korihor the Anti-Christ

Book of Mormon, Alma 30

When Korihor repented,
he scratched his confessions in the dirt.
Yet still he lay mute upon the earth.
God would not return his tongue

from the place where it lay silent.
Thus we see that if a tree brings
no good fruit, it will be hewn down
and cast into the pit.

God is ruthless and true.
Songs of praise fade
in my throat. *Thy Father,*
who seeth in secret,
shall reward thee openly.

I will speak my words in season.
I come before God with a broken neck.

Therefore shall the Lord of Hosts
send among the fat ones
leanness. He commands the heavens

to open and shut in a voice
made of fire. I will walk
in the sparks that He has kindled.
I set my face like a flint.

Excommunication

They had always followed the compass
of his teeth.

But be careful. Sound travels.

The voices come from far away,
brittle as ceramic hammers.

He can buy himself back with penance.

His girls play with their dolls
and ignore the sandwiches laid out
for lunch. For days

they do as they please. They slap
and read and pass the remote.
Rain lingers

over the rooftops
until the skylight begins

to drip. Their mother, too,
is made of water.
They watch her drain away.

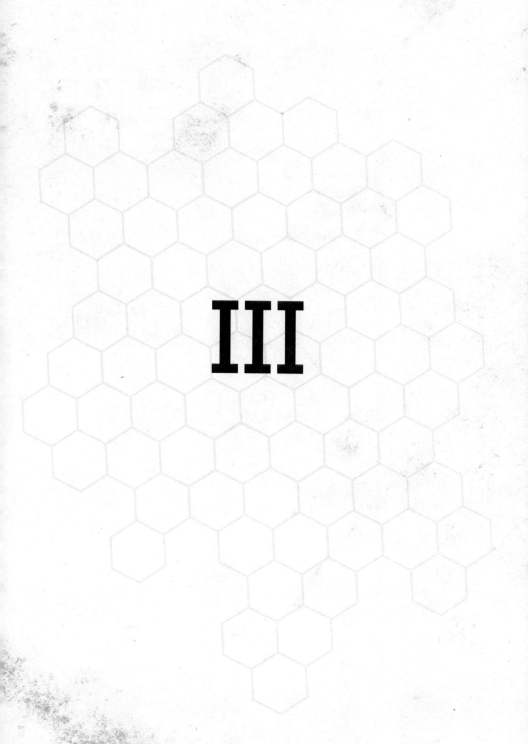

III

Our Mother Who Art in Heaven

Forgotten be thy name. Thy place
denied, thy will shackled
on earth as it is in heaven.
Give us this moon a second heart,
and forgive us our powerlessness
even as we bear those
who will one day silence us.
Endear us not to our jailers
but give us means to take up scythes
against them, for a mother
will carry her daughters
through any darkness.
For thine is the hive,
and the swarm, and the namelessness
for ever and ever amen.

What Tacoma Was

The scuffed toe of a Boeing work boot,

Puget Sound's paper-mill stench,

the asbestos cough from the Asarco plant.

A tin can that cut my thumb

every time I tried to throw it into the past. The kind

of wound that takes a full minute

to begin bleeding. A cave of evergreens

at Point Defiance Park, shutting out all light.

The stone in my soup. WIC coupons

common as pine needles, soldiers

from Fort Lewis cruising the mall for girls,

bottles of Rainier beer. The man

who held me down in the storeroom where I worked

and snarled *Don't fight me, you bitch.*

A glue so quick to bond

I had to meet my mother's eyes and tell her

she wasn't enough reason to stay.

Raped Girl's Mad Song

Christmas. A chorus of angels in the trees.
I'm the girl their hymns forgot.
The wolf, he's here—he's taken me.

He asked directions with yellow teeth.
I helped a stranger, as I've been taught.
A chorus of angels in the trees.

The dumbstruck stars have gone to seed,
dark as bone, clipped blade, a kicked-in lock.
The wolf was here—he's ruined me.

Siren, slattern, witch. Girl reduced to beast.
I touch the grafts that didn't take, knots
of neck and cheek. Weep now, angels in the trees.

I'm bruise and brimstone, dragged out to sea—
I'll have your skull for a flowerpot.
I'll hunt the wolf that hunted me.

Seven trumpets raise up my jubilee—
you're the one who will say *please*. There's not
an angel left among the trees.
The wolf, she's here. I'm her. She's me.

High School Yearbook

It's amazing how many numbers
are still connected, especially since

the land line has gone the way
of the light bulb. I keep it simple—

stick to the ones who wrote
Stay sweet or *See you later.*

Most times the voice has never heard
of Tony or Michelle. But then I'll get

a parent, voice wavering,
who sums up a life in small words:

Died in Iraq. Married and working
in real estate. Moved to Denver.

One mother says: she would
love to hear from you

I'm sure. Gives me the number
for the girl in algebra

who chewed gum and brayed
her vowels. For fifteen minutes

I talk baseball trades with the father
of the oboe soloist who believed

her crush on Jennifer
went unnoticed.

The wrong numbers tell me
to check Facebook. Best way

to find out if the prom king
sells tires. But stranger,

clipped and curt, you mistake me.
I am not calling for them.

I Must Return to the Company of Saints

One of the seventy most powerful men
        in the Mormon church lays his hands
on my head and prophesies
                that I will die.

        Wait. I'm telling it out of order.
First, I was sick. I had been
           sick for what felt like

all the years on the curtains.
        It was early autumn,
when the exodus of leaves belies

the bright sky. Specialists
        convened in teams
until my grandmother sent Elders, one
        to anoint and one to pray.

        The men lay their palms,
left over right, on my head—
        heavy as a current
pushing me under, their fingers

steady, unyielding,
rooting in my skull
to dig me out.
    The Holy Ghost speaks

    through the second man's throat:
         to be healed of my afflictions,
I must return to the arms of the Saints.
    Take up my covenants and put on
        the temple white.

        —10 a.m. sunlight fills
        my living room. Birdsong
        trills the air.

    Before he will leave, the man wants
an ending. He wants a promise
    from me, one that will grow into ivy
and take over the house.

    Miles away on the coast, my parents,
my grandparents, my sisters, my brothers,
my uncles, my aunts
    wait for God's word.
I didn't call anyone. I didn't call anyone
    until later.

Some Ungodly Hour

Forgive the hand to mouth.
Your prayers will blanket the heavens like ash.
Some of your mistakes
are forgivable. You're not the one
who gets to decide.

The night's a jimmied door.
Now the penny. Now the fuse box.
Watch the arms.
Leave quietly, making sure
to button your shirt. Let your eyes
adjust to the darkness of the first stair.

Let It Come to Pass

I learned to love the rasp, the thin neck,
the large devouring the small.

All the things we want and never got.
The salt, the sweet.

I will be the water song, you will
be the earth. Our child

will spill the sky's glass bowl
while we shape devotion out of rust.

We kneel through winter. One of us
to make the wounds

and one of us to tend them.
Our bodies mortar and pestle,

kernel and husk
rehearsing for a life apart.

Thistle

Seed pods gossip with the grass. I bleed their milk
and my hands turn black. I used to know the name

for why that happens. From a safe distance the pear trees
call me a fool. It is true that I've forgotten the name

of the first boy I kissed. I forget his lips and hair—
my heart a canvas painted over. Now I seek the name

of the star our bodies broke from, the one closest
to the throne of God. When the prophets speak its name,

the mountain will cleave in two. Only the hanged man
has ever loved me that much. We lie together and name

the nocturnal birds by their cries. I was told the greatest sin
is skin on skin, the greatest sin is hands. One name

for it is worship. But sometimes a hand is a butcher knife,
a hand is a hacksaw, a hand is teeth. Christ, it's all in the name.

The Origin of the Ampersand

My mother married the first man she ever kissed.
      To receive one gift is to be denied
            others. The bank account's

a shell casing—when the plumbing fails,
      she calls the brethren
            to come and do the best they

can. In her world, the grass is always
      overgrown and she pulls the curtains
            closed. But she knew things,

and she told them to me when I asked. Like how
      Christian missionaries tuned Anglo-Saxon
            to the Latin alphabet,

and an *E* and a *T* quick-stepped into each other's arms
      to form the ampersand. Every morning
            my mother awakens

to find the Lord has not yet taken her, and she folds
      her hands to wait. *But behold, it was appointed*
            unto man to die. She reads

the Plan of Salvation into my voice mail. *And thus we see*
    that all mankind were fallen, except an atonement
        should be made. In the pre-mortal existence,

when our spirits lived at the foot of God, she says
    we chose our earthly lives. We agreed
        to the suffering of our bodies.

But we came from a place better than this. We will return
    to better. This world, with its starlings and stones,
        is the blow that isn't real.

Judges Chapter 4

Think of the god who arranges
the scene: the wreck
of a thousand men, limbs
and skins.

Imagine Captain Sisera's
rage. As he flees the Israelite
swords, who whispers to him
that the tent of Heber
is within reach?

This god has already
called Heber away,
leaving his wife to her scarves.

When Sisera clamors
to the door of her tent,
Heber's wife wraps him in blankets,
tips a cup to his mouth.
She leads him to a soft
and guarded bed.

Think of the god who, days ago,
beckoned a workman home
with desire for drink and his
woman. So strong

was this need
that he left behind
hammer and nails.

This god has been arranging
his little pieces
on a plate. The wife of Heber
bows to him.

Think of the god who slowly
twists one commandment
into another, for the blood of it.

Imagine Sisera's stupor,
untroubled by the slain.
If he wakes, he'll
find her watching.

Consider the god
who says Kill.

Blessed shall be the name
of the wife of Heber. All the earth
shall praise it.

She gives all of her obedience
at once. She brings the hammer down.

God Made Everything Out of Nothing, But the Nothingness Shows Through

The woman you are trying to love
has finally let you see her naked.
A clutch of seagull-shaped scars
ranges over her breasts
and you have never seen anything
like it, but that only means
you haven't seen much.
You have questions and
all I can tell you is that the earth
is full of ashes. I know
it is beautiful sometimes to be violent.
That flood of surprise and pleasure
at what we are capable of
in the instant before blood
escapes the skin. We are
often told that love comes
from inside us and maybe
she tired of waiting for it.
I know it is power
to open yourself. It is power
to stand naked before a man.
And there are those of us who need

to look upon the face
of the deep, who know
that emptiness was first, before God
allowed there to be light.

Antigone Inverse

Our sister says it's the war, it's who you killed
or who you held while they were dying.
A nurse's 2 a.m. calls are becoming

as familiar as our mother's sawtooth quilt
and I am tired of covering for you
so she doesn't find out.

You came closest with the drain cleaner,
coating your throat while the rest of us
watched your nephew debut

as Peter Rabbit. My dear, I agree
that life and liberty are often
overrated, but at this point I wish

you'd either cut it out or finish the job.
At your apartment I pack your belts.
Take the rope from your tool box,

as the doctors suggest. Empty your
cabinets of bleach and pills. Then I sit
on the edge of your bed for an hour

and put it all back. Labels front,
so you can find the bottle
you want. I unlock your display case

of autographed baseballs.
Wind up and follow through.
The window above your sink shatters

on the second pitch. Then I leave you the glass.
If you want to be hurt, I'll hurt you.
I am finished clawing the earth apart

with my own fingernails. I don't give a damn
about giving you peace. The prayers
I can't stop chanting burden my tongue.

When My Mother Asks Me to Write Something Nice, I Can't

Because everything is lovelier near the end

Because I see omens everywhere, even in the curls

    of chive on my baked potato

    (especially in the curls of chive)

Because outlet malls march onward

Because I have a sword in my bones

Because I've forgotten how that pile of things

    got there, and now I owe it

    an apology

Because the month unbends into one perennial

    bad day and a sky gorged on orange and pink

    can't always hold me till tomorrow

Because crying is why we have throats

Because my right hand is full of bribes

    and the hungry children come begging for what is left

What It Is to Sin

We are born animal. Each of us
would put a javelin
in the heart of a king.

As I suspected, the moon
is mute. There are only
my human hands

and my chitin heart
to help me learn to love.

The martyr will bleed like paint dripped in water
while more blessings crowd his mouth.

I was like you once, so full
of conviction. An army
standing in readiness.

The wildness is so close. It is
bound to reach us
one way or another.

What If God Had Said It Differently

Let there be ignitions and kindling.

Let us have supermarket birthday candles,
a cigarette glow, phosphorescent flares,
a handgun's muzzle.

Let the world wrench free. Bring on
the cock-crow of atoms colliding,
arrows tipped

with burning magnesium.
Let there be cruise missiles
and burnished metal engines.

Let there be stars and cooking fires,
chandeliers and gilded walls.

When the heart quickens,
let there be dawn

over the blind trees
and the diamond sky.

THE BRITTINGHAM PRIZE IN POETRY
Ronald Wallace, Series Editor

Old and New Testaments • Lynn Powell
Carolyn Kizer, Judge, 1995

Brief Landing on the Earth's Surface • Juanita Brunk
Philip Levine, Judge, 1996

And Her Soul Out of Nothing • Olena Kalytiak Davis
Rita Dove, Judge, 1997

Bardo • Suzanne Paola
Donald Hall, Judge, 1998

A Field Guide to the Heavens • Frank X. Gaspar
Robert Bly, Judge, 1999

A Path between Houses • Greg Rappleye
Alicia Ostriker, Judge, 2000

Horizon Note • Robin Behn
Mark Doty, Judge, 2001

Acts of Contortion • Anna George Meek
Edward Hirsch, Judge, 2002

The Room Where I Was Born • Brian Teare
Kelly Cherry, Judge, 2003

Sea of Faith • John Brehm
Carl Dennis, Judge, 2004

Jagged with Love • Susanna Childress
Billy Collins, Judge, 2005